How to Drop Everything and Travel Around the World!

How to Do It, Where To Go & Why It's Cheaper Than You Think

By Dagny Taggart

Disclaimer

The information provided in this book is designed to provide helpful information on the subjects discussed. The author's books are only meant to provide the reader with the basics knowledge of a certain language, without any warranties regarding whether the student will, or will not, be able to incorporate and apply all the information provided. Although the writer will make her best effort share her insights, language learning is a difficult task, and each person needs a different timeframe to fully incorporate a new language. This book, nor any of the author's books constitute a promise that the reader will learn a certain language within a certain timeframe.

Table of Contents

Preview Of "Learn Spanish In 7 DAYS! - The Ultimate Crash Course To Learn The Basics of the Spanish Language In No Time"

Dedicated to those who love going beyond their own frontiers.

Keep on traveling,

Dagny Taggart

Introduction
Are You Ready? Let's Go On An Adventure!

Look up. Do you see an airplane flying overhead? Can you picture yourself on it, soaring over the world, away from your home, from your miniscule material objects, and into a new world, somewhere you've never visited before?

The United States sees nearly 90,000 planes take off and land throughout its borders. Somewhere, right now, someone is going on vacation.

Why isn't that someone you?

We all make excuses: I have a job, I have kids, I have parents to support, I have bills to pay, I have a girlfriend who's afraid of flying, it's too expensive, I have a pet dog, I have a strict phone contract, I've never travelled before. I'm scared.

You can justify your stagnancy any way you like, and justify it well. All the above are perfectly valid reasons to say to yourself, "Jeez, you know, I just can't take the time off right now, maybe next year."

Maybe next year, next year, next year…

We're all running out of next years.

Here's the thing: someone can watch your dog. Someone can watch your parents. You're afraid to lose your job of 10 years? With 10 years' experience, you can get another one when you get back. You can you're your contract, rent out your fully furnished house and bring your kids. (Many travelling parents do.)

And then there's the cost. Oh, the cost! Look, travelling isn't nearly as expensive as you might think. Or, rather, it doesn't *have* to be—it depends hugely on a number of factors, which we'll detail in this book.

I just finished a four-month trip from East Asia to North America for around $7,500. That includes airfare, hotels, transport, food—everything. I paced through the Taj Mahal alone, slept in a Bedouin camp in the middle of the Jordanian dessert, choked on tamarind-spiced street food in Kolkata, partied with musicians from Belgrade, and hitched rides across Iceland.

Now I want to show you how you can do it, too.

Sure, if you stay exclusively in European hotels, you'll spend more money than you if spend more time in Southeast Asia. If you buy your tickets early and manually, your whole round-the-world ticket can be bought for maybe $3,000, with stopovers in two dozen countries. You just need to know the right tools.

A disclaimer: there's no *science* to travel. It really is more of an art, a fluid movement from one place to another. You can never predict every variable, and we can't tell you what your trip is going to be like, smell like, or look like.

In short, this book is written purely from well-researched statistics and anecdotal evidence. Many of the anecdotes will come from my own trip. Not all of what you read will necessarily hold true for you—certain crazy cheap flight sales (I once bought a ticket from Kuala Lumpur, Malaysia to Phnom Penh, Cambodia for $20 *after taxes*) come only once or twice a year.

So the title of this book—"How to *Drop Everything* And Travel the World"—should be considered in the long-term. It's true that if you have a mortgage, children and bills, it's hard to drop everything and travel in the same week. Round-the-world trips take lots of planning, certainly weeks, probably around two or three months, sometimes a year or two. Think about the kind of trip you want to take now, and convince yourself of its reality by buying tickets early in advance—it'll be cheaper for you in the long run, and it'll force you to make a promise to yourself that you cannot easily break.

Are you ready? **Let's go for it!**

Chapter 1
Making Up Your Mind To Travel

Why travel? This is the quintessential question every traveler asks him or herself. Why bother spending hideous gobs of money to do something with, really, no tangible benefit? Something that only provides us with memories and thoughts, maybe a few trinket souvenirs, but not with any more money or functional experience?

Hundreds of the world's best travel writers have tackled this question. Pico Iyer, one of the greats, opens his essay "Why We Travel" with the following words:

> *"We travel, initially, to lose ourselves; and we travel, next, to find ourselves. We travel to open our hearts and eyes and learn more about the world than our newspapers will accommodate. We travel to bring what little we can, in our ignorance and knowledge, to those parts of the globe whose riches are differently dispersed. And we travel, in essence, to become young fools again -- to slow time down and get taken in, and fall in love once more."*

If you need more convincing than that, try reading some of the world's most classic travel literature: Paul Theroux's *The Great Railway Bazaar,* Jon

Krakauer's *Into the Wild*, Jonathan Steinbeck's *Travels with Charley*, Jack Kerouac's *On the Road*. These are stories wherein the protagonists venture off into unknown territory at all points in time, seeking new experiences and viewpoints to redefine their lives. Reading any one of them can convince you to travel.

Lots of people think they shouldn't travel because they're afraid to, or they're living on a shoestring budget. Let's clarify a few things here.

Reasons you should *not* travel: don't travel if you've already made up your mind about the world, if you dislike other cultures, or if the outside world doesn't especially interest you.

Reasons you *should* travel: if you're frightened of change, if the thought of other countries makes you uncomfortable, if you're in a life slump, or if you've found yourself saving more money than you need with no real plans to spend it.

You'll notice I excluded a large portion of people who have long since made up their minds to go exploring. What's that, you say? You have a natural curiosity about the world? You enjoy eating new, different foods? You get excited at hearing capital cities of countries you've never been to? You like roughing it?

Yeah, well, don't worry; you know you're going to travel. I don't need to convince you.

There are a lot of ways to drop your life and travel the world, and after you've decided to simply do it, you have to figure out how. You can find any of the myriad jobs sitting out there for native English teachers, many of which don't require any sort of certification; you can find a volunteer organization and ship out to Africa or Southeast Asia; you can spend a bit more time finding an overseas job, either at a business or on a cruise ship; or you can, as this book with detail, simply pack up your things and go.

This book presumes that you have no excuse to go other than the fact that *you want to.* I want to take that nugget of desire and help you flesh it out into something real, something you can take with you as you journey forth into new lands and reference if you're in a bind. I want to teach you how to travel if you don't already know.

So, back to the question at the top of this chapter.

Why travel?

A better question: Why *not*?

Chapter 2
Getting Your Sh*t Together Before You Leave

Getting up and going is not as easy as we'd like to think. There are so many things to consider at home that we don't even think about. Sometimes we may quietly wish that we could steal away in secret, just vanish, fall asleep and wake up in a new country, and send a letter once a month to a friend: "Hey, I'm okay, just trekking the jungles of Borneo. Give my love to Cathy."

Of course, it's not so easy. Modern travel is nothing like what we can only imagine it was for those who wrote the brilliant travelogues listed in chapter 1. We have an inescapable connectedness that binds us to society no matter where we are, and we have the ease of travelling by bus, taxi, train and plane to virtually anywhere in the world, provided we can afford it.

Basically, we can do way more than Steinbeck and Kerouac could. And with that development comes a cost, a trade-off from the innocence of travelling somewhere truly undiscovered, adventurously unsafe, as Paul Theroux so often did, and replacing that sense of danger with a keen awareness of the world, unlimited precedents and social media, which, no matter how far you are, as long as you have the Internet, ensures that you're never really very far at all. (If you don't have the Internet, well then—you're in the thick of it then.)

So the question is no longer, "How do we drop off the map altogether?"

But rather, "How do we disconnect from society?"

First, tell people. Tell them you're going. Make announcements on Facebook and Twitter and Tumblr and whatever you use; if people know you're going, you're making a public promise to do it. No backing out. That helps, if you start to get cold feet.

Second, sell your stuff. There are too many of you readers right now for us to address every single situation, but let's start with the main one: your stuff.

George Carlin said it best: "A house is just a place to keep your stuff while you go out and get more stuff." Get rid of some of it! You don't need most of it, honestly. One of the joys of travel is that it forces into perspective your needs from your wants. Travelling with just a backpack invites you to realize that, wait a second, all I really *need* are a few clothes and money for food and a roof at night. Heck, if you travel with a tent you don't even need the roof.

Hold a garage sale. If a garage sale is too old-fashioned (or, you know, it's still winter) then try eBay, Craigslist or a comparable website. Or ask your friends if they need material goods that you're getting rid of. A long-term travel plan tends to invigorate change in one's life, and returning to the same old, same old can be a real downer. If you've been meaning to get a new lawnmower and your friend is looking for one, whatever—just give it to him. You won't be using it, anyway. If your friends won't take some old shirts and socks, try donating them. Anything that turns this opportunity into a chance to start your life anew. Many travelers report that when they come home they feel the need to do away with old clothes they never wore anyway. The benefits of selling your stuff are obvious: your items won't collect dust sitting at home, and you could collect a few extra bucks for your trip. (Remember: "a few extra bucks" could be a week's worth of food in India.)

If you're not willing to part with much, then toss it in storage. There are storage units everywhere that charge weekly or monthly rates to hold your things while you're gone. If you want to save the money, and you don't have too much to worry about, consider asking some friends or family members if they'll take a box or two.

Let's examine some bigger problems than just old rags and toys. If you own a car, you must find yourself in a financial and sentimental bind. It depends on what kind of car you own. Remember: everything that can be sold can be bought again. Just because you sell this vehicle that's taken you thousands of miles over 10 years doesn't mean you can't find another one when you get back. If it's in good condition and you can get a few thousand dollars out of it, it's a better idea to sell it than to let it sit uselessly somewhere, gaining age and rust. If it's an older car and you don't think you could get much cash out of it, there's no harm in letting it sit around and wait for you—assuming you're coming back to this city at all.

Of course, you might not own your car outright. If you're paying monthly fees on a lease, ask around to see if any of your friends or family members would be willing to proverbially take the lease over for a time. They don't have to dish out all your payments, but they could pay 50 percent of what you pay, cut your costs and keep the thing running while you're away. The nicest thing about this arrangement is that it would mean you wouldn't have to worry about it when you return—you'll have your car, and you've saved some cash.

If you own or rent a house, consider what I mentioned briefly above, renting it out. There are dozens of companies that help homeowners rent out their fully-furbished homes to strangers under a contract for a set amount of time. (Some people actually do this full-time, and spend their time travelling or between other homes.) If you do this, you should take precautions when inviting others to live at your place—take photos, sign agreements, and hire someone to check in before and after your tenants arrive to make sure everything is still in place.

Depending on the length of your trip, you could also consider outright selling your home. Lots of couples who've gone on year-long trips (or longer) found it cheaper to stay in inexpensive guesthouses in South America. This is the kind of commitment that thrills people who would never consider it—why not consider it? There will be houses on the market when you return, don't worry.

Next, let's talk jobs. If you hate your job—perfect! Quit it. Problem solved. When you come back, you'll have a whole host of new opportunities, and though it might take some time, you can get back in the swing of things quickly, especially by drumming up old connections.

But let's say you enjoy your job, and don't want to lose it. Before you worry what your boss will say, or resign yourself to resigning, you should ask your employer about a sabbatical, or a leave of absence. Sabbaticals aren't often well advertised, but if you've been with your company for a long time, you may have some clout to toss around. It's worth investigating. Meanwhile, with a leave of absence, one of the biggest benefits most people rarely think of when it comes to unpaid leaves is that you might be saving someone else's job: if your company is downsizing, your boss may be thrilled at the opportunity to cut costs with employees volunteering to leave. You can part ways with the understanding that, in a year, things may be looking different for the company. There's no guarantee they'll be able to hire you back, but finding jobs has always been about networking, and at the very least your boss may feel bad and be a useful reference.

Also remember that when you go on a round-the-world trip, you won't come back the same. No, you won't return to the world a Walter Mitty-style rugged traveler, but you might discover a secret passion abroad that forces you to reconsider your career path. You may not *want* the same job when you return. There's no shortage of stories online that tell of travelers on a career break who found it helped clear their minds.

Next, let's talk about safety and health care. Maybe you have health insurance, maybe you don't; regardless, you won't abroad, unless you buy travel insurance. If you punch in "travel insurance" to Google and hit search, you'll find no shortage of blogs and magazines promoting the heck out of it, often with links to their own travel insurance partners. This ebook is affiliated with no such insurer, and can verify that thousands of travelers go across the world without travel insurance every month. Don't feel pressured into buying it.

That said, if you're travelling with kids, engaging in extreme sports or going to an especially dangerous part of the world like central or eastern Africa, you should definitely consider it. There are too many options to list here, but know that coverage for stolen cameras, broken legs and unexpected typhoons are all different, with differing costs. Take some time to into what your options are before leaving home.

Immunizations fall under this category as well, and are a good idea if you're travelling, again, to Africa or Southeast Asia. But know that most problems people encounter on the road aren't viral, and the viral or bacterial infections that do strike travels most often are not preventable. Dengue fever is significantly more common than malaria, and there's nothing you can do about it—except guard against mosquitoes. Meanwhile, malarial pills can be very expensive, and induce drastic side effects like drowsiness or bowel problems.

I bought malarial pills before spending two months across Cambodia, India, Laos, Borneo, Thailand, Bali and Java. The pills are still sitting in my desk, unopened and dusty. Once I discovered the side effects, I realized that I wasn't even going to the wildly dangerous parts of these countries—I was travelling to the big capital cities, where malaria is virtually unheard of, and rarely straying into the jungle alone. Also, it was autumn, meaning the wet summer months had all passed.

So before you rush out to buy every pill and get immunized with every needle, consider where you're going, what time of year you're going, and whether it's really worthwhile. That said, if you feel like protecting yourself against typhoid or Hepatitis B, it's never a bad idea to be immunized—even in your own country.

Lastly, let's talk about cats and dogs. The sentimental attachment we grow towards our pets can often dissuade us from travelling; the thought that someone needs us is a very compelling reason to stay home and take care of them. You can, of course, travel with your pet—but it's difficult. Not all hotels are accepting, and walking down the streets of Yangon clutching your cat is less than ideal. Not to mention the pet fees that airlines pile on if you plan on taking a lot of planes. The fact is, not all dogs behave so well when straddling the earth's atmosphere hundreds of miles above the sea.

The easiest solution is the least forgiving: give them up, if only for a time. Usually everyone has a friend or family member who's willing to take a cat for a few months, especially if you offer to compensate them a bit. If you can't find someone, or you're going for longer than just a few months ("Please take my cat for a year" is a pretty hefty request), you might just need to find a new home for your pet. Put up ads and ask around, and you'll find it's no trouble to find a new loving someone who's able to take care of Mittens for the rest of her life.

After all, if travel teaches us anything, it's how to say goodbye.

Chapter 3
The Essential Guide to Packing

When I travelled the world for four months, I took a single 35-litre backpack. Nothing else. It fit in every carry-on compartment on every airplane. I never checked a single piece of luggage, and I never found myself lacking. When friends I visited in Europe saw what I'd brought, they'd be baffled. "Where's your stuff?" they'd ask. "Is that all?"

The truth is, you really don't need a lot to travel. Travel is a terrific excuse to minimize yourself, pare down your valuables into what you really need and what you can live without.

A disclaimer for this chapter: the time of year you travel from and to will totally and completely affect what you bring. If you're travelling from summer into winter, like I did from August until January, be prepared to throw out your well-worn summer shorts sometime in October and buy a new winter jacket on the road. If you don't want to throw out any clothes, you can always mail them home, or at least home to a friend or family member. It would be a joy to plan a trip that only involves warm weather, hopping from one hemisphere to another, but odds are it won't happen, and you'll have to plan ahead.

I began my trip in Indonesia with three quick-dry t-shirts, one button-down collared shirt, two long-sleeve shirts, one pair of shorts, one pair of lightweight summery pants, one thin sweater, swim trunks, one breathable sports jacket and six pairs of socks and underwear. I only brought one pair of shoes (runners) and one pair of flip-flops (necessary if you plan on staying in hostels with grimy shower floors), and all this fit in my one 35-litre backpack—although, if I needed, I could unfold my smaller compact neoprene backpack, which folded up nicely into the size of my fist. This is all in addition to technical doo-dads like my SLR camera, iPad, smartphone, toiletries, sunblock, notepads and travel documents.

Here are some essential clothing rules to follow when packing for this sort of trip:

1) *Buy quick-dry clothes.* These things are incomparably brilliant and useful. They wick away sweat so you don't wind up with clingy damp cotton t-shirts at the end of the day (which sometimes don't even dry after a full night, or which you have to quickly pack away into your bag and then grow all musty and smelly), they're impeccably lightweight, and they fold up smaller than cotton shirts do. In short, they're built for travelers. If you're concerned about looking like a lame dad in oversized, brightly-

colored t-shirts, know that big retail brands like The Gap, H&M and American Apparel all sell these sorts of things.

2) *Don't pack wool, pack layers.* If you're preparing for a winter trip, the worst use of space is to fill your bag with thick puffy lambs wool sweaters. My bag could have fit maybe three before I'd run out of space. Instead, try layering: one t-shirt, two long-sleeve shirts, a thin sweater and a lightweight jacket together combine to make a heck of a stronger armor than just one shirt and one sweater. The nice thing about layering is that you can adjust your layers on the weather—if it's a cold morning in Berlin, start with all your layers, bring a small backpack, and shed them as you warm up, or as the sun comes out.

3) *Pack less than you think you'll need.* If you're the type who finds it hard to get rid of things forever, you might be troubled to know that such things happen on the road: laundry gets lost, bags get stolen, or winter sets in and you need to do away with your shorts. Pack less than you think you'll need, so you can buy as you go. Though it may be trouble if you're an XL size shopping in Southeast Asia, you'll want to predict that you're going to be buying a lot more than

you expect—especially once you realize how cheap vintage clothes are in Bangkok.

4) *Leave room for more.* I filled my backpack to the brim with what I brought (in truth, I think I pared down my belongings as well as I could—but a 40-litre backpack would have been a better investment), and when I wanted to buy a souvenir, I could barely fit it in. It's always a good idea to have a bit of leeway. Even if you don't buy souvenirs, you may find that you need to reach something at the bottom of your bag one day—say, I don't know, purely hypothetically, that iPad keyboard you bought for $30 specifically for this trip—and spend the next 20 minutes unpacking and repacking your bag to retrieve it.

5) *Ditch the jeans.* Jeans are terribly bulky, not especially warm, and will almost 100 percent rip in the crotch by the time your trip is done. They're just not very versatile. That said, my girlfriend brought her skinny black jeans along, and after a bit of frustration with them, cut them off and turned them into shorts. Some travelers have also reported enjoying the comfort in a variety of locations. It's personal preference, but generally khakis and long johns are a better idea.

6) *Wear what you'll be doing.* If you're planning on camping and hiking a lot, by all means forgo fashion sense and buy those cargo pants. If you're banking on enjoying Western European capital cities, two pair of shoes might be justified. Ultimately, the decision is yours for what makes sense given your trip.

The next big question, after clothes, is technology. This depends on how dependent you are on gadgetry. I've travelled with and without a smartphone, and can testify from personal experience that having a virtual offline map has saved me uncountable hours of grievance. Google Maps has an offline mode, or else CityMaps2Go is an excellent and cheap app that offers offline GPS tracking and, when connected to the net, can automatically download relevant Wikipedia pages for whatever you're nearby.

Lastly, let's talk books. Books are huge. You have no idea how huge a book is until you pack it. Tablets and e-readers are a godsend. That said, you may feel a bit first-world self-conscious when busting out your iPad on the Kolkata-New Delhi train, especially when surrounded by impoverished Indians. If you can handle your privilege and stomach the stares, it'll save you good space in your backpack.

Chapter 4
Where Are You Going? Let's See Some Ideas!

I read a study in a journal, *Applied Research in Quality of Life,* that discovered that people are happier when they're planning a trip. Not *on* a trip, mind you—just planning one. The very hope and promise of travel, the optimistic essence of *what could be*, lifts our spirits, even if it's a year away; we naturally cling to the idea of other worlds as being somehow greater than our own, more relaxing and warm.

So what are you waiting for?

The most fun I had was spending three months planning my trip. Researching customs, making hit-lists of foods to try, gawking at photos of palaces and ruins I would soon see, waiting to pounce on airline deals as soon as they popped up.

As a crash course in where to go, I'm going to help you decide what countries or regions might interest you based on a criteria of factors.

1) You're frugal, and can mentally afford to rough it. You enjoy the hostel vibe, can live without a bit of privacy if it means you can catch a glimpse of the world's most fascinating thousand-year-old temple ruins;

you hate spending more than $4 on a meal and you're not afraid of running into a few other travelers—have a few cheap local beers and wake up for a hike the next day. What I'm describing here is **South and Southeast Asia**—a backpacker's paradise. Great for inexpensive outdoor adventures like zip-lining, water rafting and mountain biking, Southeast Asia excels at spicy food, a welcoming tourist environment and some of the most beautiful colonial French architecture in the world. Bangkok is an obvious starting point, while Vietnam and Cambodia are rising stars; Bali is a cultural oddity anywhere in the world. If you want to explore a lesser-known area, the secluded Myanmar is your best bet.

2) You want something like what's described above, but with a bit of European flair—without the European costs. You're more interested in contemporary culture, big cities, modern architecture and street art. You can handle spicy food and are fascinated by colorful slum life, but you're not willing to sacrifice the classic wild outdoors, events like horseback riding, mountain climbing, camping in national parks. Maybe you want to put your rusty Spanish to good use? Yes, you're the best fit for **South and Central America**. With loads

of Spanish and Portuguese traditions permeating every meal and social cue, not to mention the wild Amazon jungle or Patagonia mountain range, this continent might be your best bet. Colombia is a rising star in the region, not nearly as dangerous as everyone thinks; Buenos Aires is one of the world's leading culture capitals; and travelling the full length of Chile is a famous backpacker route.

3) You enjoy the outdoors, but want to immerse yourself fully in a world where you don't understand the language. You're less concerned with price and more concerned with authenticity—it bothers you to see locals contriving their way of life to suit your need. You like to look at pictures in a menu, shrug, and point to one at random. You aren't super into cafes, but you enjoy architecture and tradition, and rich cultural history that is miles away from what's familiar. If you're up to learning a whole new set of cultural codes, and emphasizing politeness, **East Asia** is your gambit. China, Taiwan, South Korea, Mongolia, Japan— though all hugely distinct, this region of the world gravitates towards cultural reservation and precision over rambunctious nightlife and outdoor adventures. Sure, you can still climb the

Great Wall or summit any of Korea's many mountains, but it's more common to enjoy the city nightlife—bike around Beijing's streets and stop for a greasy bowl of chow mien, or swing by a Tokyo jazz club and enjoy a one-of-a-kind craft beer.

4) You enjoy other cultures, but want to keep it reasonably safe. You prefer to stay close to home, but still want to travel overseas. More than anything, you enjoy spending a bit of money—this is your trip, after all; it's a once-in-a-lifetime thing, so why not splurge a little? You prize cafes and grandiose architecture, symphonies and high art. You want to see what all the fuss was about when you studied Michelangelo and Picasso, and are curious to see the leading artists of the modern world, and indulge in some of the greatest, cleanest cuisine on Earth. Yes, this is **Europe** for you, and though East and West Europe will differ greatly, not to mention the customs within each extremely diverse country, the fact that you can ride the train from London to Skopje, Macedonia means that your experience can be wrapped up tightly. If you do plan on splurging in Europe, consider a balance: don't just stick with Germany, France, Spain and Italy; branch eastward to Budapest for a bowl of cherry

soup, or see the budding street art world of Warsaw, or awe at the cleanliness of Vilnius, Lithuania, a world-class city that sprung up overnight.

5) You're a daredevil, and a humanitarian. Rules don't keep you down. You don't care as much for famous buildings or fancy food; what defines a trip for you are the people you meet and the experiences you share, and going the touristy route wouldn't cut it. You're not afraid to sleep in a tent, and the thought of working abroad excites you. But most importantly, you want to see for yourself what the Third World looks like—not just the images on TV, but the real people who live and fight to eat every day. You want to see it for yourself, and understand ancient traditions of tribes struggling to survive in our globalized world. For the politically minded, **Africa** is a good bet. Safety precautions trump all here—best to avoid Somalia and the Democratic Republic of the Congo, for example, and if you're a solo traveler (especially female) you may want to reconsider your specific destinations. Homosexuality and public displays of affection are often not tolerated in public, but if you play it safe, you can learn a tremendous amount about Ethiopia's coffee history, South Africa's

racially divisive past and Tanzania's endangered wildlife. Generally North and East Africa are a bit sketchy these days, but venture to West Africa—Senegal, Ghana, Cote d'Ivoire, Burkina Faso—to discover a much more civilized and contemporary world than you might expect.

6) You want to speak English, plain and simple. You don't want to fuss over new cultures so much as you want to take it easy, go on a long, meditative road trip and discover an easily accessible land. You probably also want to camp or hike a great deal, and eat food that's mostly familiar but just a little bit off—French fries with gravy and cheese curds, or a comforting twist on Mexican food. Most of all you want wide expanses of wilderness, rugged travel, where you're less concerned with the outside world than you are with testing your own personal limits. You needn't venture farther than **North America, New Zealand or Australia**, where there are bound to be enough new experiences without facing a huge culture shock. Each state, province and territory offers a wealth of knowledge about its own traditional tribes and customs, as well as fully modern cities and towns. Anyone will tell you: the bustling 24-hour life of New York is nothing like the quaint Alaskan

capital of Juneau, and in between you can explore Canada's finest Rocky Mountains or the Maritime east coast.

7) You want to go somewhere *no one* you know has gone before. You want to disappear into the mountains, flee into a rural community and struggle to communicate. You can handle being a true nomad, and appreciates the modesty of Muslim lifestyles. You aren't afraid of border security and can live without the Internet for as long as you'd like. You have a tent and a strong spirit and want to come back with truly unique photos. **Central Asia** is your destination, my friend—not for the faint of heart, but the central –stans (Tajik, Uzbek, Kyrgyz, etc.) offer totally bizarre and still undiscovered opportunities. They live in harsh conditions and political oppression, often overlooked by the global community. The good part? No one's come back with something bad to say.

8) You're politically or religiously geared, explorative and not afraid to totally submit to new cultures. You embrace new experiences and don't have an attitude of bringing your own emotional baggage along with you—you like to integrate, but also study a culture. You're pensive and care

about where the world is heading. You're less concerned with the outdoors, don't care at all about drinking or partying, and more concerned with understanding differences—probably a poli-sci major, or religious studies. In this case you want to head to the **Middle East.** Though the news depicts the region as a constant hotbed of dangerous extremist Muslim activity, in reality the Middle East is mostly peaceful and extremely modern. The United Arab Emirates, Qatar and Bahrain are some of the most modern, lavish destinations in the world, with sleek amenities to help you survive in the dry desert climate. Israel is a thoroughly European-style country. Jordanians are friendly, with Petra being one of the world's leading archeological experiences. Iran and Saudi Arabia have stricter social laws, but penetrating their borders offers tremendous insight into the world of an ancient religion that birthed many of our modern traditions.

I hope that helped shed some light on your possible options. The next part is up to you. I of course left out specifics from loads of regions—the Oceanic islands of Fiji and Kiribati, the Indian subcontinent, the differences in African cultures, exotic Caribbean islands—but these broad descriptions above will have to suffice for now.

When you're planning your trip, be sure to try and map a logical route—obviously no zigzagging from Iceland to Mexico to Italy. Also try and find logical stopovers when booking flights. Often flying between more obscure cities requires a stopover in a major hub, and it can be cheaper (or at least the same price) to buy two separate flights—one to the hub, and one from the hub to your next destination. Major hubs include Frankfurt, Germany; Amsterdam, Netherlands; Guangzhou, China; London, UK; Buenos Aires, Argentina; and Chicago, USA.

Hopefully by now you have some idea of *where* you want to go. Next we'll take a look at something much trickier—*how* to go.

Chapter 5
Worldwide Travel Tips: Where to Go, Sleep, and Eat

No one can prepare you, truly, for your own personal adventure.

But damned if I can't try.

There are certain rules to the road, as it were, of travelling long-term. No two countries are alike, but many countries share cultural ticks and customs that are best researched beforehand. I can't detail all of them, but I can give you some tips as to what to look for.

Speaking of tips—tips! One of the biggest international cultural faux-pas is tipping culture. Many Asian countries don't have it at all; Europeans round up; North Americans leave 15 percent. Check online, or don't be afraid to ask your cabbie or waiter what tipping culture is, rather than risking leaving an inappropriate one. They might be bashful, but usually they won't lie.

Be aware of gender roles. It goes without saying that making out in Mecca is a no-no, but you might be surprised by some countries' rules about PDA. (In Laos, for example, it's technically illegal for a foreigner to have sex with a local. Remember that next time you're in a Vientiane nightclub.) Not all countries are gay-friendly, and many Asian countries disapprove of showing too much skin. The government of Vienna recently banned making out on subways, as well as loud cell phone conversations and smelly food, which is at the same time brilliant and good to know before you go.

Be religiously conscious. Many Buddhist temples require visitors to leave off their shoes before entering, and touching heads is also considered improper. In Muslim countries, be prepared for the world to shut down Fridays between 12 and 2 p.m. for weekly prayer. (This really stuck it to me and my girlfriend when trying to catch a bus out of Brunei—nothing was open. Not restaurants, not stores, and certainly not the bus station.)

Remember the kind of gastronomical world you're entering into. Don't go to China if you hate noodles. A lot of equatorial cultures love spicy food, but locals understand that you might be less accustomed to it. This awareness applies to alcohol as well. For instance, in South Korea, it's quite rude to deny a drink offered to you by someone older. In Iran, of course, you can't even buy liquor.

Be prepared for how you're going to spend your nights and travel time. In Southeast Asia, where the tourist infrastructure is among every country's largest economic booster, anyone can show up on a standard day, buy a bus ticket and ride to the next city. In overpopulated countries like China and India, this is hardly the case—train tickets sell out months in advance. Even if you're planning to play it by ear and improvise as you go along, it's good to know your odds of success before you show up.

Travel will also vary wildly on your budget. Those with comfortable budgets can afford to fly short domestic distances and save hours of travel time, whereas trains will typically cost about half of what it costs to fly (unless you're in Europe or North America, in which case it will cost maybe the same, but will be more of an adventure anyway), while the cheaper option will always be bussing it, and the cheapest being to simply hitchhike or bike and really take your time.

If you're considering a proper round-the-world trip, you're probably on some sort of budget. That means you'll be travelling overland a lot. This is actually a really fun way to travel; you meet locals, or at least see what they're really like, have time to plan what you'll do in the next city, and decompress from the last one. You should consider utilizing your travel time with overnighters—there are sleeper buses and trains that might cost a little more than a daytime route, but will save you the cost of a hotel. Overnight rides differ everywhere— Argentina is famous for swanky flatbed buses, while I once rode one across Java wherein we switched buses at 2 a.m. without our knowledge and we were too late and wound up standing up, holding onto a grimy black bar from then on until 6 a.m. while the driver played Indonesian karaoke hits and '90s AQUA music videos. Then again, that was a $5-ride. We should all be so lucky.

The only real moral there is to try and know what you're getting into, and know that the cheaper you go, the certainly less comfortable you will be. But if all you want to do is get from point A to point B, you can do it.

Going through North America or Australasia means renting a car is a terrific idea. Be sure to get an international driver's license or equivalent with the country you're going to. Being freely on the road, able to stop and camp anywhere you want (maybe you've got an RV? Even better) has a way of making travelers feel more free than anything else. In countries like Iceland, where a six-hour bus costs a ludicrous $100, renting a car is a very, very fine option indeed.

Ultimately, the lesson here is to do your homework. Like I said earlier: studies have proved that simply planning a trip makes people happier. So do your research. The last thing you want is to show up to the airport and realize you don't have the visa you didn't know you need. (It's happened to me, and it's an awful, gut-wrenching feeling.) So take the time and learn up before you go.

Then, when you come back, you can call yourself a certified expert. Isn't that a nice perk?

Chapter 6
Tackling Issues on the Road (Where Would We Be Without Surprises?)

Safety first, they say. You will stumble and startle on your trip, no question. You may be scammed, robbed, swindled, lied to, cheated, poisoned, bitten by a malarial mosquito, kidnapped by the cartel, or you might simply miss your flight.

Just kidding. Sort of. Very little of this will probably happen to you—any of it can, but it's no more likely than getting hit by a car while jaywalking. The fact is that the myth of dangerous travel is mostly unfounded. With common sense telling you to avoid walking alone through dark alleys at night, and to not enter sketchy neighborhoods, and to not flash your SLR and iPad at every opportunity in the Third World, you'll mostly likely be fine.

The fact is that you're probably not going to the world's most truly dangerous countries—Somalia, Libya, Iraq. Every country issues travel warnings for extremely dangerous countries, while most countries that are merely publicly perceived to be a bit sketchy—like Colombia, Cambodia or Pakistan—are, in fact, perfectly safe, as long as local customs are adhered to, and common sense is followed.

What's more likely to happen are basic problems, like traveler's diarrhea, bed bugs or pick pocketing. These are relatively mild problems and easy to solve, and shouldn't be allowed to ruin your trip.

As a general rule, big cities are more dangerous than small towns. Pickpockets run more rampant and gangs stake out territory (if that's even a thing where you're going). But that said, any time you're isolated means you're surrendering yourself to chance. One of my best friends was travelling through Nicaragua, and was held up by two guys who pulled giant rusty machetes out from under their shirts on a quiet beach. There's no telling what can happen.

Generally, the more developed the country, the better the police will be at assisting you. And in countries struggling to gain international clout, you may find "tourist police boxes" scattered around city street corners, as in Indonesia and Cambodia. But for the most part, cops can't help tourists much—once a guy's stolen your cash, he's gone.

But don't let it ruin your trip. Here are a few tips to help you prevent the worst from happening. We'll start with crime.

Keep your valuables hidden. Only walk around with your large SLR camera if you have it wrapped around your arm securely; even then, you're showing off your wealth. Likewise with your smartphone or tablet—only pull it out if you need to text or check the map, but don't use it like a constant map, following it and keeping your eyes downcast. Jewelry, obviously, is another giveaway for wealth. One of the benefits of wearing quick-dry t-shirts and cargo pants is that you won't look particularly rich.

Next, divvy up your cash. Always keep two wallets, divide your cash and cards between them, and keep them separate—one in your bag, one on your person; or one on your person and one at the hotel. That way, if worst comes to worst, you'll still have something. The old eggs-in-one-basket trick. Some travelers will swear by subtle money belts, too, to be kept on the inside of your clothes like a furtive fanny pack; I never used one, but it sounds like a good idea.

Lastly, try not to get too drunk, wherever you are. You're out to have a good time, sure, but if you're stumbling back to your hostel at 4 a.m., you're likely to find trouble. (That said, I have a friend who backpacked through South America extensively for a few months on mostly a beer binge; he got mugged twice, but the first time he didn't even realize what was going on, stared the man down, and the offender got scared and ran away. So, I don't know, it's the luck of the draw?)

Keep locks on your bags when you're not around, and never leave valuables unattended. Hotels usually have safes at the counter—use them. And if you ever fall asleep in public (maybe in an airport, or on a night bus), then try and loop your bag around your arms, or use it as a pillow.

More common than thievery, though, is scamming. Common transit hubs are the worst—unregulated taxis waiting outside airports and train stations are known to try and finagle a quick easy buck from any weary traveler who's willing to just get to their hotel. In India, a 20-rupee ride can cost 200 rupees before you start haggling. Keep your wits about you, even if you're tired. As a general rule, avoid the first offer that springs up before you.

Lastly, food poisoning. Possibly the most common of them all. Our stomachs settle after years of digesting the same foods again and again; they become used to a certain standard. Even if the food is perfectly clean and well-prepared, a new type of meat or especially greasy, fatty foods can spoil a vacation by forcing you into the bathroom more often than you'd like.

In general, especially regarding street food, play to what looks right. If there's a lone vendor woman with no customers, there might be a reason. I always abide by three rules: eat at places that are busy (the food will be fresher), local (they know what's good) and cheap (to avoid being overcharged). Go where the crowds are, and you'll probably be fine.

That said, it's always a good idea to carry diarrhea pills with you. Bring some from home if you're skeptical about overseas remedies.

It's also a good idea to bring earplugs, cold medicine or a blindfold if you're a sensitive sleeper. I was never one to bring an inflatable pillow, but lord did I envy those who did.

Chapter 7
Let's Cut To The Chase: How Much Will It Cost Me? (Hint - It's Cheaper Than You Think)

Travel can be not just freeing—also free. There's no shortage of guides with titles like "Europe on a Shoestring" or "See South America for $30 a Day", and while a lot of cases sound like people willing taking extreme measures, or who have connections across the world, that isn't always the case.

They're called "travel hacks"—ways to hack the system in your favor to score cheap or free flights, inexpensive meals, discount accommodation , the whole shebang. If you work remotely, it's possible to travel for under $20,000 per year—meaning you could feasibly travel constantly and work from wherever you are, be in the beaches of Bali or the Tanzanian bush.

But to enjoy these cost savings, you have to be willing to relax your expectations a bit. If you go the route of low-cost carrier airlines, you'll have to accept no TV screens or free meals. (Although "free" is a misnomer—any time you fly with a major carrier, you're paying double the price of a base fare for a meal.) Likewise, with hotels, obviously you can find cheaper accommodation by accepting dirtier hotels—or roughing it entirely and camping out in a tent for free each night—but even if you go the hotel route, using online services like Hotwire match you with hotels slashing prices by as much as half on a last-minute-only basis—only, the catch is, you don't know what the hotel is until you make your purchase. So you can never have it all at once.

You also want to make sure you're not sacrificing your enjoyment for the sake of cost. What's the point of travelling to Paris if you're going to be miserable sleeping in filthy hostels and eating supermarket sandwiches? The occasional splurge is necessary. You just have to figure out what to splurge on. Remember that even if, say, windsurfing is something you've always wanted to do, but it costs as much as three nights at a $15-per-night hostel, it may *seem* like a lot of money in that specific context, but in reality $45 is nothing compared with the flight you took to get there.

Start by keeping a lookout for discounted plane fares. Once or twice a year, usually in off-seasons, airlines (especially wide-reaching low-cost carriers like Ryan Air or Air Asia) will hold massive sales. I used Air Asia to fly from Korea to Indonesia for $150 (usually it's $300), from Indonesia to Brunei for $60 (usually $100), from Malaysia to Cambodia for $20 (should be $90), and from Bangkok to Kolkata for $60 (normally at least $200). That's because I spent months checking websites on a weekly basis before the trip actually started.

Saving up air miles is another excellent way to go. With enough patience, you can earn well over enough to fly anywhere for free. One travel blogging couple reported that in their first year of travel hacking, they saved around 1.5 million miles from credit card bonuses—enough for 25 round-trip fares to Europe.

When it comes to hostels, you'll have to gauge for yourself how low you're willing to go. Some rooms in Varanasi, India cost $3 per night, but you couldn't pay me $20 to sleep in them. My partner and I settled on average costs with optimum hygiene—something like $15-$25 per night (divided by two), and we always checked the rooms first.

Use Agoda or Hotels.com to investigate the costs of hotels and restaurants where you're going, and consider an average of three meals a day; do the math and calculate what else you can afford (like souvenirs or public transit), or what your budget should be, and this will give you a rough idea of long you can afford to stay there.

If you're going the dirt-cheap option, try Couchsurfing.com, a network of open-minded people who set up their homes as de facto guesthouses for travelers on a budget. You'll get to meet fascinating locals or expats, make new friends and return with wacky stories. It's very hit or miss. I stayed with a fellow in Berlin who kept dried bloody tissues on his bedside table, and I later stayed in my own luxurious room under the roof of an Icelandic helicopter pilot.

Other good options, if you're used to a certain level of comfort, are sites like VRBO and Airbnb.com, which organize apartment swaps or a Couchsurfing-style atmosphere for a reasonable fee.

When you're looking for food, consider street food. I mentioned my three rules above, but they warrant repeating: eat at places that are busy, local and cheap. In countries like India and the Philippines, they're the best way to go. Also, always take a browse through local supermarkets. It's not ideal for every meal, but packing a lunch is a great way to keep costs down and see what locals eat on-the-go. For example, while exploring the side dishes of any South Korean restaurant is an imperative part of the experience, it's not unfair to call pre-packaged rice triangles for under a dollar, found in every corner store, an authentic culinary experience. Pair it with banana milk and garlic potato chips and you've not only spent less than $4 on lunch, but you've also eaten a distinctly Korean meal that you'd never find anywhere else in the world.

Be sure to scan the streets and local papers for free cultural experiences, as well. My best memory of Manila is stumbling on a free outdoor dance performance in Rizal Park on a Saturday, with families picnicking everywhere, munching on soft yam rolls and mango slices, watching the dances against the backdrop of a golden sunset. Many European cities are known to offer free museums—London's Tate Modern is among the finest in the world, and has free main exhibits all year-round; the Louvre in Paris is free a few times a month; Berlin has no shortage of walk-in modern galleries throughout its hipper districts.

Always give public transit a shot before relying on taxis. Taxi drivers are more likely to scam you, especially if they claim their meters are "broken" or if they offer a number off the top of their head. Taking a local bus might seem daunting at first, but don't be afraid to ask someone who seems trustworthy (popping into a local store is a good idea) and hopefully they'll speak enough English to help you get on your way. That said, it's important to measure cost versus enjoyment again: just because you can ride the subway in New Delhi for 10 cents doesn't mean being crammed up closer against sweaty armpits than you ever thought you could be is worth it. Three dollars is still cheap for a taxi.

It's also important, *before* you take your trip, to calculate how much you plan on spending on all the little things—things you may not realize you need to spend money on. Ryan Air can offer unbeatably cheap flight fares from Paris to Edinburgh, but they only fly out of Paris's Beauvais International Airport—which is, as many critics have noted, at an hour outside the city, hardly in Paris at all. That's an extra 16 Euros on top of that 30-euro flight—50 percent more than you were expecting. (As an aside, Ryan Air is also notorious for strict baggage allowances and charging you unexpectedly when you arrive at the gate. Check your bag weight before you go.)

Also consider laundry costs, whether Internet will always be free or if you'll want to invest in a local SIM card, that you'll often need to buy bottled water, how much entrance visas cost and airport fees cost (if you're American, you can't enter China unless you pay $170; some airports, as in the Philippines, charge you an "airport maintenance fee" on your way out of around $20), and how much ATMs charge around the world—my bank tacked on $5 to every debit withdrawal I conducted abroad, whether I withdrew $20 or $100. Credit cards usually add on a varying percentage depending on how much you take out. Do your research.

Guess what the bottom line here is? As with everything, it depends on your trip—and your budget. Depending on where you go, you can manipulate the world to fit whatever you want out of it. If you're looking for a spa weekend, take it in Malaysia instead of Italy. If you're cautious but curious to indulge in street food, play it safe in Bangladesh and wait until Germany's hearty bratwurst scene.

The important thing is that you find a way to make it work. One of the most beautiful parts of travelling is that you create your own lifestyle, not beholden to your normal social self. Whatever your budget, you can make it work.

Chapter 8
Staying Sane Abroad

When I travelled the world for four months, I was with my girlfriend. I admit: it wasn't always easy. A few times we needed space, and agreed to go our own ways and meet back in an hour. But we were lucky, insofar as we travel well together: we can both rough it, we enjoy taking chances on street food, we like renting bikes and escaping from the summer heat in quirky museums.

But it won't work all the time. Whether you're travelling alone, with a partner, a friend or in a group, if you're with them for a long period of time, you'll need to stay sane. You'll need a break, a compromise, a moment to yourself.

Let's look at solo travel first. It's the most adventurous, the most spiritual way to go—just you alone with a backpack, literally against the world. You'll necessarily meet new people and try things you'd never try back home. You won't feel pressured to be the same person. You can really change yourself—put on a new mask and see how it feels.

But you might also get lonely. Long bus rides stop being agreeably meditative after about 15 minutes, and you might miss your loved ones back home.

Thankfully, social media makes it possible to feel like you've hardly left at all—between Facebook and emails, you can stay connected all the time. Some hardcore travelers may see this as a sign of weakness, but remember: your mother will probably want to know where you are if she can help it.

Staying connected also means you can take a break from travelling, hit the pause button for an hour and stow away in an Internet café while you write a quick email or blog post. If you bring a smartphone or tablet, it's even easier—especially if you're spending a lot of time on trains and buses. Most hostels offer free Wi-Fi, and almost every hotel does.

Travel burnout is normal—don't see retreating to the Internet or the comforts of social networking as a weakness. See it as a respite from your respite. If your device has Skype, see if any of your friends or family want to pop online for 20 minutes and say hi. It can go a long way to keeping your head in the right space.

And then there's blogging. Should you start a travel blog? It's a huge time investment, especially if you want to try and make it a reputable travel source. On the plus side, a blog can help you keep in touch with your family and friends on a much easier scale—it's like a mass email.

On the downsides, a single blog post—at least the way I did it—took a good hour (at least) to write, edit and upload photos for. You almost certainly will not make money from this venture, either. But it can be a nice memento for yourself of your trip—cheaper than souvenirs, and more personal.

But staying sane on the road alone is more difficult than just delving online. You'll be tempted to take strangers up on their offers, or reject them automatically out of fear that they're untrustworthy. This constant state of worry can create a real, palpable sense of isolation in a traveler—like you're alone in the world, and everyone is out to cheat you.

Just remember that you're the best judge of your actions. If you're uncomfortable taking a ride with someone you just met, don't. You can walk away from this creepy Vietnamese driver and literally never see him again in your life. Try not to attract too much attention to yourself, especially as a tourist; dress normally and blend in, as well as you can, locally. Often the fly-on-the-wall approach is more interesting for solo travelers, anyway, who aren't confident in their ability to just go out and meet people. You can learn a lot about a culture and yourself simply by watching people be themselves. When you're alone, this is much easier.

The other advantage to Skyping or keeping up with social media is that you can make your movements transparent. Yes, it may feel like cheating a bit—letting your father know your itinerary, even from thousands of miles away—but if something happens to you, it's important that someone have an idea of where you were. Otherwise you may wind up with your arm trapped under a boulder in a canyon while everyone assumes you're safe.

While you don't want to be perceived as a sucker, it's also an emotionally draining experience to glare at anyone who tries to make chitchat. It's true, experienced scam artists will often lure you in with impeccable friendship, sometimes even spending a whole day with you before slipping something in your drink or sliding your wallet out from your back pocket. But there are also many decent people out there, and half the fun of travelling alone is meeting them. Start cautious and suss out personalities.

But let's say you're travelling with a partner—boyfriend, girlfriend, husband, wife. Ways to stay sane will be totally different. Coping with another person for 24 hours a day, several weeks at a time can be exhausting.

It's crucial to establish rules early. My girlfriend and I agreed that if one of us ever needed time apart, we would say so and the other should not take offense. We also understood what the other one probably would and would not want to do—neither of us care for expensive tourists sites, so we skipped paying $40 to reach the top of the Tokyo Skytree, but we both love jazz, so we knew we'd want to find a small downtown club that night.

Make sure your travel styles mesh. One partner might be more willing to rough it in a crappy hostel if the price is right, while the other could be less keen, demanding at least a modicum of privacy and hygiene every night. Some love the efficiency of overnight trains, others hate the discomfort of them.

Know these things before leaving. Ask your partner what they prefer to spend money on—rate food, accommodation, experiences and comfortable transit on a scale from most to least important. It's possible you won't travel well. Are you an indoor person, or outdoor? Do you like to eat quickly for energy, or enjoy a long and unique meal? Are you more likely to get up at 6 and take advantage of the daylight hours, or wake up and stay up late? Do you like to plan meticulously ahead of time, or play the whole thing by ear?

Some couples set ground rules strictly because they know they won't necessarily agree: one partner chooses the day's events on Mondays and

Wednesdays, the other on Tuesdays and Thursdays, etc. It won't work for everyone, but it might for some.

Other couples find travelling together ruins the relationship. They get along fine at home, but can't deal with their partners constant idiosyncrasies on the road. When you think about it, travelling together is as serious as moving in together
.
Make sure you have a similar idea of what your trip will look like, and never make decisions individually—significant others tend to resent that. (Unless, of course, it's a grand romantic surprise, in which case, well done.)

The other way to stay sane as a couple is to check each other's levels of energy. What drains one personal mentally may revitalize another. Don't be afraid to suggest staying in while your partner goes out for a night tour; just because one person's tired doesn't mean the other should feel bad for wanting to see more. As long as both parties are on the same page, you should be fine.

Lastly, remember: travel doesn't have to equal stress, but it also doesn't mean you'll be constantly carefree. The fundamentals of travelling together are the same for travelers as for relationships at home: a solid foundation of trust and appreciation can resolve most issues before they even arise. Just be honest with yourself and your partner, give yourselves space when you need it, take time to yourselves as a couple every so often, and be conscientious of each other's needs.

With all this said and done, there's no reason your life partner can't also be your travel partner.

Conclusion
What Are You Doing Here? Bon Voyage!

That about sums it up! Thank you so much for reading this book. I hope you found it helpful enough to decide where and how you want to travel from now on.

If there's one last takeaway message, it's this: Define your own style. The bottom line from every chapter is that people are different; they travel differently, they enjoy different things. No one, not even I, can tell you what will work on the road. That's the whole deal of traveling: finding yourself!

And really, that's the beauty of travelling. You won't know what works for you until you face it yourself. Travel is all about self-development and expression, learning what you enjoy, discovering new foods for yourself, new art forms, new fashions and new languages. Maybe you'll hear Dutch for the first time and think to yourself, "I want to learn that language."

That's why we travel. Not just to see the world through our own eyes, but to see ourselves through the world's eyes.

Thanks for read, and good luck on your journey!

To your success,

Dagny Taggart

Preview Of "Learn Spanish In 7 DAYS! - The Ultimate Crash Course To Learn The Basics of the Spanish Language In No Time"

Are You ready? It's Time To Learn Spanish!

Most people are daunted by the idea of learning a language. They think it's impossible, even unfathomable. I remember as a junior in high school, watching footage of Jackie O giving a speech in French.   I was so impressed and inspired by the ease at which she spoke this other language of which I could not understand one single word.

At that moment, I knew I had to learn at least one foreign language. I started with Spanish, later took on Mandarin, and most recently have started learning Portuguese. No matter how challenging and unattainable it may seem, millions of people have done it. You do NOT have to be a genius to learn another language.   You DO have to be willing to take risks and make mistakes, sometimes even make a fool of yourself, be dedicated, and of course, practice, practice, practice!

This book will only provide you with the basics in order to get started learning the Spanish language. It is geared towards those who are planning to travel to a Spanish-speaking country and covers many common scenarios you may find yourself in so feel free to skip around to the topic that is most prudent to you at the moment. It is also focused on the Spanish of Latin America rather than Spain. Keep in mind, every Spanish-speaking country has some language details specific to them so it would be essential to do some research on the specific country or countries that you will visit.

I will now list some tips that I have found useful and should be very helpful to you in your journey of learning Spanish. I don't wish you luck because that will not get you anywhere- reading this book, dedicating yourself, and taking some risks will!

Important note

<u>Due to the nature of this book (it contains charts, graphs, and so on), you will better your reading experience by setting your device on *LANDSCAPE* mode!</u>

Language Tips

Tip #1 - Keep an Open Mind

It may seem obvious but you must understand that languages are very different from each other. You cannot expect them to translate word for word. *'There is a black dog'* will not translate word for word with the same word order in Spanish. You have to get used to the idea of translating WHOLE ideas. So don't find yourself saying, *"Why is everything backwards in Spanish*?" because it may seem that way many times.   Keep your mind open to the many differences that you will find in the language that go far beyond just the words.

Tip #2 - Take Risks

Be fearless. Talk to as many people as you can. The more practice you get the better and don't worry about looking like a fool when you say, *"I am pregnant"* rather than *"I am embarrassed,"* which as you will find out can be a common mistake. If anyone is laughing remember they are not laughing at you. Just laugh with them, move on, and LEARN from it, which brings us to our next tip.

Tip #3 - Learn from your Mistakes

It doesn't help to get down because you made one more mistake when trying to order at a restaurant, take a taxi, or just in a friendly conversation. Making mistakes is a HUGE part of learning a language. You have to put yourself out there as we said and be willing to make tons of mistakes! Why? Because what can you do with mistakes. You can LEARN from them. If you never make a mistake, you probably are not learning as much as you could. So every time you mess up when trying to communicate, learn from it, move on, and keep your head up!

Tip #4 - Immerse yourself in the language

If you're not yet able to go to a Spanish-speaking country, try to pretend that you are. Surround yourself with Spanish. Listen to music in Spanish, watch movies, TV shows, in Spanish. Play games on your phone, computer, etc. in Spanish. Another great idea is to actually put your phone, computer, tablet and/or other electronic devices in Spanish. It can be frustrating at first but in the end this exposure will definitely pay off.

Tip #5 - Start Thinking in Spanish

I remember being a senior in high school and working as a lifeguard at a fairly deserted pool. While I was sitting and staring at the empty waters, I would speak to myself or think to myself (to not seem so crazy) in Spanish. I would describe my surroundings, talk about what I had done and what I was going to do, etc. While I was riding my bike, I would do the same thing. During any activity when you don't need to talk or think about anything else, keep your brain constantly going in Spanish to get even more practice in the language. So get ready to turn off the English and jumpstart your Spanish brain!

Tip #6 - Label your Surroundings/Use Flashcards

When I started to learn Portuguese, I bought an excellent book that included stickers so that you could label your surroundings. So I had stickers all over my parents' house from the kitchen to the bathroom that labeled the door, the dishes, furniture, parts of the house, etc. It was a great, constant reminder of how to say these objects in another language. You can just make your own labels and stick them all over the house and hope it doesn't bother your family or housemates too much!

Tip #7 - Use Context clues, visuals, gestures, expressions, etc.

If you don't understand a word that you have heard or read, look or listen to the surrounding words and the situation to help you. If you are in a restaurant and your friend says, "I am going to ??? a sandwich." You can take a guess that she said *order* or *eat* but you don't have to understand every word in order to understand the general meaning. When you are in a conversation use gestures, expressions, and things around you to help communicate your meaning. Teaching English as a second language to young learners taught me this. If you act everything out, you are more likely to get your point across. If you need to say the word *bird* and you don't know how you can start flapping your arms and chirping and then you will get your point across and possibly learn how to say *bird*. It may seem ridiculous but as I said, you have to be willing to look silly to learn another language and this greatly helps your language communication and learning.

Circumlo... what? This is just a fancy word for describing something when you don't know how to say it.   If you are looking to buy an umbrella and don't know how to say it, what can you do? You can describe it using words you know. You can say, it is something used for the rain that opens and closes and then hopefully someone will understand you, help you, and maybe teach you how to say this word. Using circumlocution is excellent language practice and is much better than just giving up when you don't know how to say a word. So keep talking even if you have a limited vocabulary. Say what you can and describe or act out what you can't!

SECTION 1: THE BASICS

Chapter 1
Getting the Pronunciation Down

Below I will break down general Spanish pronunciation for the whole alphabet dividing it into vowels and consonants. One great thing about Spanish is that the letters almost always stay consistent as far as what sound they make. Unlike English in which the vowels can make up to 27 different sounds depending on how they are mixed. Be thankful that you don't have to learn English or at least have already learned English. There are of course some sounds in Spanish that we never make in English and you possibly have never made in your life. So get ready to start moving your mouth and tongue in a new way that may seem strange at first but as I keep saying, practice makes perfect!

The charts on the next page will explain how to say the letter, pronounce it, and if there is an example in an English word of how to say it I put it in the right column.

Vowel Sounds

Vowel	How to say the letter	How to pronounce it in a word	As in...
a	Ah	Ah	Taco

e	Eh	Eh	Egg
i	Ee	Ee	Easy
o	Oh	Oh	Open
u	Oo	Oo	Book

Consonant Sounds

Consonant	How to say the letter	How to pronounce it in a word	As in…
b	beh	similar to English b	
c	ceh	k after *a, o,* or *u* s after *e* or *i*	cat cereal
ch	cheh	ch	cheese
d	deh	a soft d (place your tongue at the back of your upper teeth)	three
f	efe	F	free
g	geh	h before i or e g before a, o, u	him go
h	ache	silent	
j	hota	H	him
k	kah	K	karaoke
l	ele	like English l with tongue raised to roof of mouth	
ll	eye	Y	yes
m	eme	M	money

n	<u>e</u>ne	N	<u>n</u>o
ñ	e<u>nye</u>	Ny	can<u>y</u>on
p	<u>p</u>eh	like English p but you don't aspirate	

Consonants continued

Consonant	How to say the letter	How to pronounce it in a word	As in…
Q	<u>k</u>oo	k (q is always followed by u like English)	<u>q</u>uilt
R	<u>e</u>re	* at the beginning of a word you must roll your r's by vibrating tongue at roof of mouth * in the middle of a word it sounds like a soft d	
rr	<u>e</u>rre	roll your r's as mentioned above	
S	<u>e</u>se	Like English s	<u>s</u>orry
T	<u>t</u>eh	a soft English t, the tongue touches the back of the upper teeth	
V	<u>v</u>eh	like Spanish b	<u>b</u>oots

Consonants continued

Consonant	How to say the letter	How to pronounce it in a word	As in…
w	dobleveh	like English w	water
x	equis	*Between vowels and at the end of a word, it sounds like the English *ks*. *At the beginning of a word, it sounds like the letter *s*.	*box *sorry
y	igriega	like English y	yellow
z	seta	s	six

Note: If you're not sure   how to pronounce a word,   one thing you can do is type it in *Google translate* then click on the little speaker icon in the bottom left corner to hear the correct pronunciation.

To check out the rest of " Learn Spanish In 7 DAYS! - The Ultimate Crash Course To Learning The Basics of The Spanish Language In No Time", **go to Amazon and look for it right now!**

Ps: You'll find many more books like these under my name, Dagny Taggart.
Don't miss them! Here's a short list:

- Learn **Spanish** In 7 Days!
- Learn **French** In 7 Days!
- Learn **German** In 7 Days!
- Learn **Italian** In 7 Days!
- Learn **Portuguese** In 7 Days!

- Learn **Japanese** In 7 Days!
- Learn **Chinese** In 7 Days!

- Learn **Russian** In 7 Days!

- Learn Any Language FAST!

- How to Drop Everything & Travel Around The World

About the Author

Dagny Taggart is a language enthusiast and polyglot who travels the world, inevitably picking up more and more languages along the way.

Taggart's true passion became learning languages after she realized the incredible connections with people that it fostered. Now she just can't get enough of it. Although it's taken time, she has acquired vast knowledge on the best and fastest ways to learn languages. But the truth is, she is driven simply by her motive to build exceptional links and bonds with others.

She is inspired everyday by the individuals she meets across the globe. For her, there's simply not anything as rewarding as practicing languages with others because she gets to make friends with people from all that come from a variety of cultures. This, in turn, has broadened her mind and thinking more than she would have ever imagined it could.

Of course, as a result of her constant travels, Taggart has become an expert on planning trips and making the most of time spent out of what she calls her "base" town. She jokes that she's practically at the nomad status now, but she's more content to live that way.

She knows how to live on a manageable budget weather she's in Paris or Phnom Penh. She knows how to seek out the adventures and thrills, no doubt, lying in wait at any city she visits. She knows that reflection on each every experience is significant if she wants to grow as a traveler and student of the world's cultures.

Because of this, Taggart chooses to share her understanding of languages and travel so that others, too, can experience the same life-altering benefits she has.

Printed in Great Britain
by Amazon.co.uk, Ltd.,
Marston Gate.